Level 1

# The Church Musician

by
David Carr Glover
and
Carl Ricker

# FOREWORD

THE CHURCH MUSICIAN — Level I is a piano method designed to follow logically the Primer Level. It continues to present a concise step by step approach to the fundamentals of music through the use of familiar and new religious music. It should be reinforced with other correlated materials available at this level. Should the student not complete all of the correlated materials in Level I and be ready to proceed with Level II — THE CHURCH MUSICIAN, the materials are so designed to carry over into the first part of this level.

For additional materials to supplement THE DAVID CARR GLOVER CHRISTIAN Piano Library, THE DAVID CARR GLOVER Piano Library is recommended.

A complimentary thematic piano Teacher's Guide of all GLOVER, BELWIN-MILLS materials is available from the publisher upon request. A thematic Organ Teacher's Guide is also available.

## MATERIALS CORRELATED WITH "THE CHURCH MUSICIAN" — Level I

# Contents

# Music Fundamentals

The following music fundamentals were given in the *Primer Level* of the *David Carr Glover Christian Piano Library*. They are given again for reference and review.

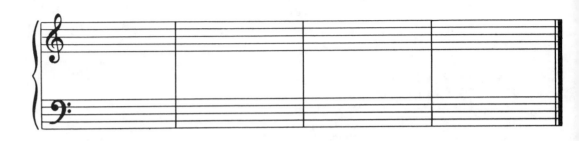

**GRAND STAFF**

## Keyboard and Notes

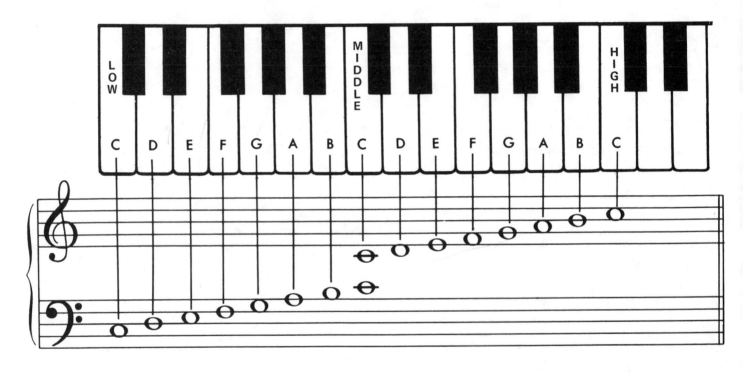

## Time Values of Notes and Rests in $\frac{4}{4}$ Meter

| | | | |
|---|---|---|---|
| **QUARTER NOTE** | ♩ = 1 Beat | **HALF NOTE** | ♩ = 2 Beats |
| **DOTTED HALF NOTE** | ♩. = 3 Beats | **WHOLE NOTE** | 𝅝 = 4 Beats |
| **QUARTER REST** | 𝄽 = 1 Beat | **HALF REST** | ▬ = 2 Beats |
| **WHOLE MEASURE REST** | ▬ = 4 Beats ($\frac{4}{4}$) | **WHOLE MEASURE REST** | ▬ = 3 Beats ($\frac{3}{4}$) |

# Time or Meter Signatures

Two Beats for each Measure. Quarter Note receives 1 Beat.

Three Beats for each Measure. Quarter Note receives 1 Beat.

Four Beats for each Measure. Quarter Note receives 1 Beat.

**LEGATO** — Play in a smooth and connected way.

**SLUR** — A curved line over ⌢ or under ⌣ a group of notes.

**PHRASE** — A musical thought. It is indicated by the SLUR.

$f$ (FORTE) means loud.

$p$ (PIANO) means soft.

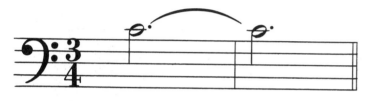

A curved line connecting two notes on the same line or space. Play the first note only and let it SOUND for the value of both notes.

**RIT.** (RITARDANDO) — Play gradually slower.

**STACCATO** — Play detached.

**SHARP**  — When placed before a note, play the next key to the right.

**FLAT**  — When placed before a note, play the next key to the left.

# Key Signatures

Key of C MAJOR

**Key Signature: No sharps or flats.**

Key of G MAJOR

**Key Signature: F sharp.**

Key of F MAJOR

**Key Signature: B flat.**

You are now ready for a new book CHURCH MUSICIAN THEORY — Level I.

FDL 549

## TO THE TEACHER:

In the *Primer Level of THE CHURCH MUSICIAN* of the *David Carr Glover Christian Piano Library,* **Page 13,** the following was stated regarding phrasing . . . .

"A curved line, SLUR ⌒ over or under a group of notes is called a phrase mark.

A PHRASE is a musical thought and is played in a smooth and connected way . . . . LEGATO. Lift the wrist gently at the end of a phrase making a small break in the sound without interrupting the rhythm."

At this point to further amplify on the technic of phrasing, the first note of a phrase is usually played with a down-arm touch. The last note is played with an up-arm movement which shortens the tone duration slightly.

For the most part throughout *Primer Level and Level I of THE CHURCH MUSICIAN,* the authors have used the rest to indicate the PHRASE release believing that this exaggeration helps the students to See, Hear and Play more musically.

Phrase marks (SLURS) are seldom indicated in a hymnal. The words of the hymn may be used as a guide for proper grouping of the notes into phrases. Whenever a standard hymn is used in this book, phrase marks will not appear.

# Correct Hand Position

**Below is a picture of a correct hand position. Note the curved fingers supporting the arched hand. Remember the finger tips must be firm at all times.**

# C Major Five Finger Position

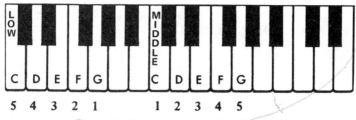

# C Major Etude

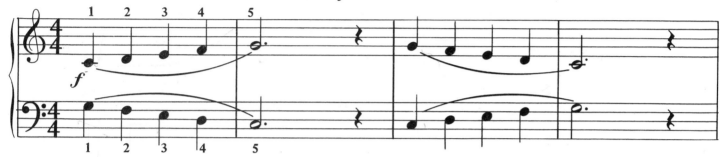

*Repeat playing* **p**

# Left Hand Accompaniment C Major*

**The following left hand notes are played together and accompany the melody played by the right hand.**

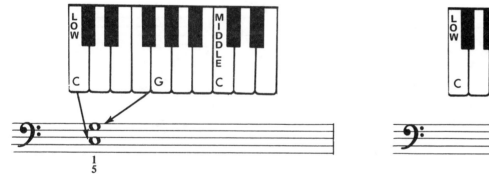

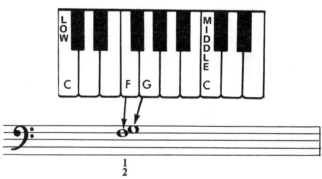

*This accompaniment will be used over and over again. You will use it for songs in many keys. Play it at least five times each day.

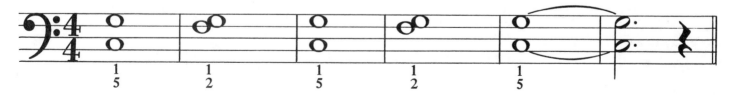

**\*TEACHER:**

For the more mature student, it is suggested that all three notes of the I and V7 chords be used. The teacher could have the student draw in the missing notes for each chord. This is recommended for all keys.

You are now ready for a new book CHURCH MUSICIAN REPERTOIRE — Level I.

# Two-Note Phrases

The following exercises are presented to further help you master the technic of phrasing. CAREFUL ATTENTION TO CORRECT HAND POSITION AT ALL TIMES.

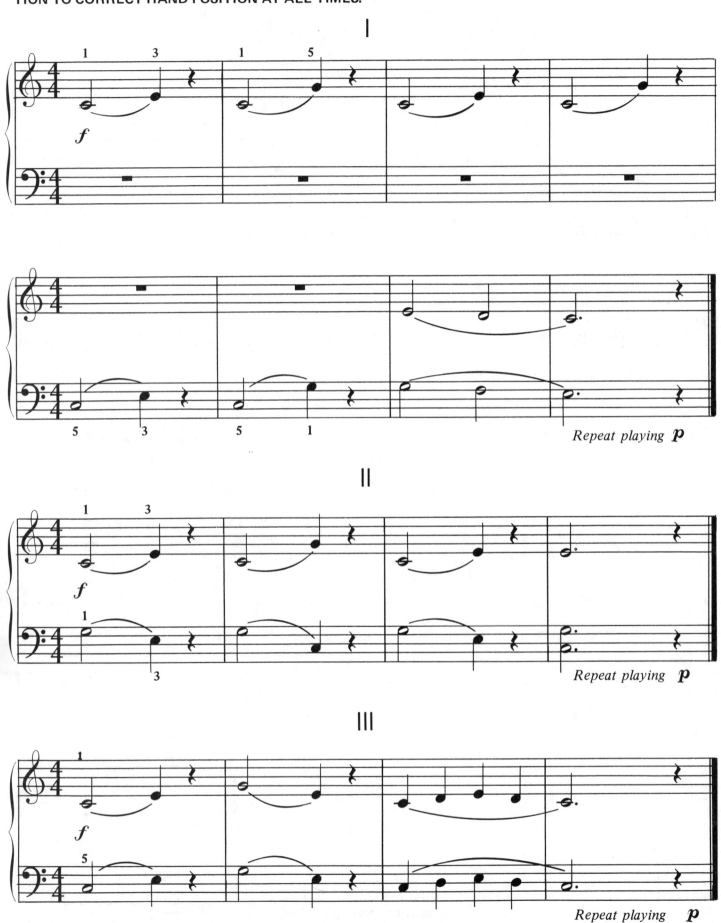

I

Repeat playing *p*

II

Repeat playing *p*

III

Repeat playing *p*

The DAMPER PEDAL sustains tones:

PRESS DOWN      HOLD      LIFT

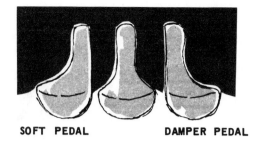

SOFT PEDAL      DAMPER PEDAL

Before studying THE BELL RINGER, review LEFT HAND ACCOMPANIMENT C MAJOR on page 7.

# The Bell Ringer

(Two Note Phrases)

Moderato (at a moderate rate of speed)

GLOVER

*f* Down up, Down up, ring the bell.

Triangle

Ding dong, Ding dong, it does tell,

Sun - day morn - ing now is here,

Ring out, Ring out, loud and clear.

FDL 549

## F Major Five Finger Position

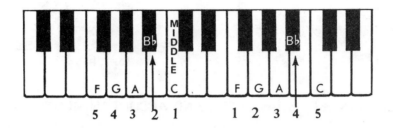

## *F Major Etude*

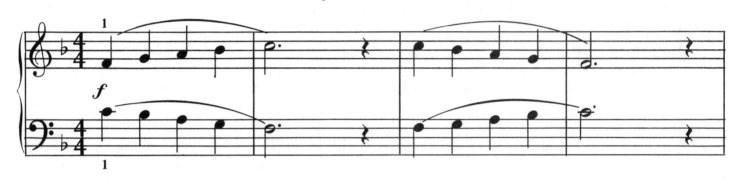

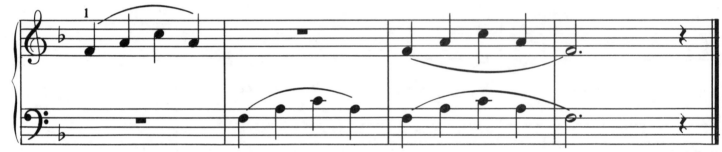

*Repeat playing* **p**

## Left Hand Accompaniment - F Major

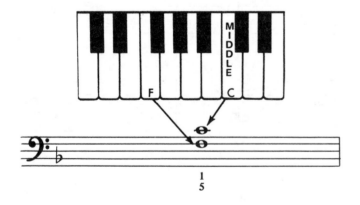

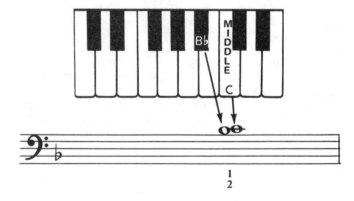

**Practice the following accompaniment before playing Holy Bible, Book Divine.**

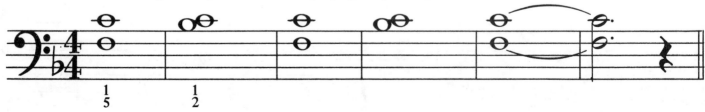

The word AMEN is used to close most hymns. Should the hymn have more than one stanza, usually the AMEN is used after the last stanza only. The use of the word AMEN which means "So be it" is an expression of reverent approval.

# Holy Bible, Book Divine

JOHN BURTON

Wm. B. BRADBURY

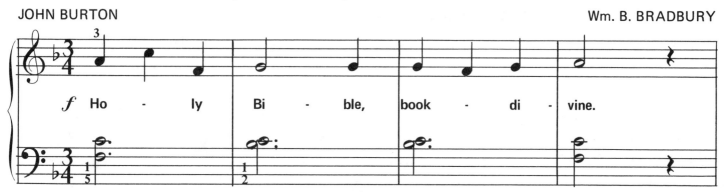

Ho - ly Bi - ble, book - di - vine.

Pre - cious trea - sure thou - art mine;

Mine to tell me whence I come;

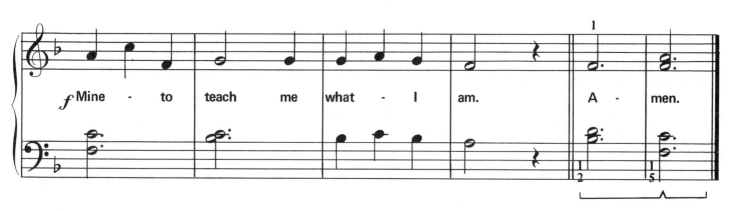

Mine - to teach me what - I am. A - men.

---

## Prelude

A Prelude is a composition usually played before the worship service. It may be repeated all or in part depending on the time remaining prior to the service. More than one Prelude may be used.

---

## Staccato

A dot above ♪ or below ♩ a note means to play detached—not legato. This is called STACCATO.

*mf.* Mezzo Forte - Moderately Loud.          *mp* - Mezzo Piano - Moderately Soft.

# *Prelude in F Major*

This piece begins on the fourth beat of the measure. The missing first three beats will be found in the last measure.

RICKER

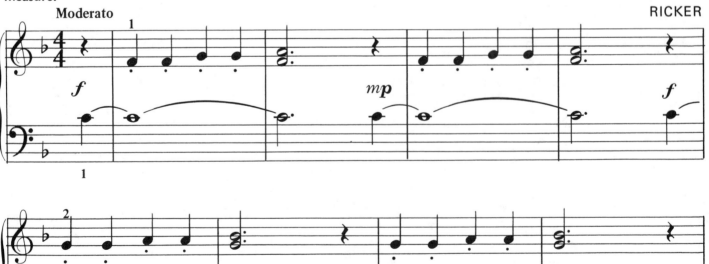

## G Major Five Finger Position

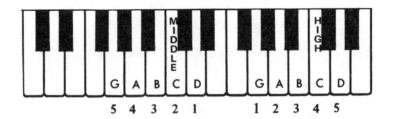

# *G Major Etude*

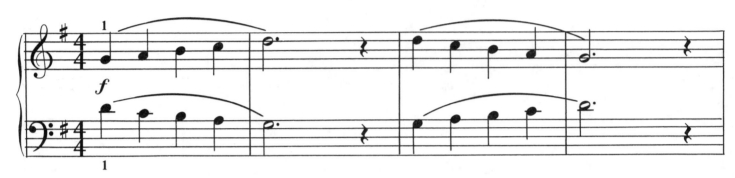

*Repeat playing* **p**

## Left Hand Accompaniment - G Major

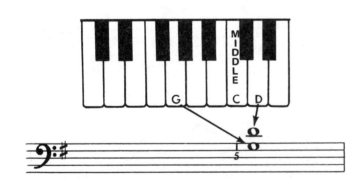

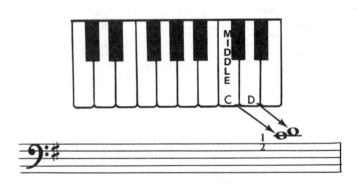

**Practice the following accompaniment before playing** *Lord Of All Being.*

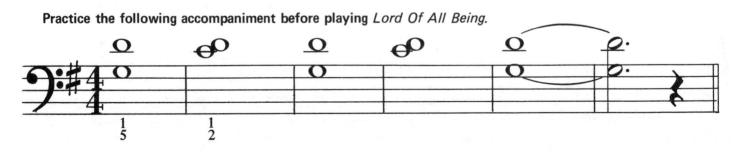

# Lord Of All Being

OLIVER W. HOLMES

VIRGIL C. TAYLOR

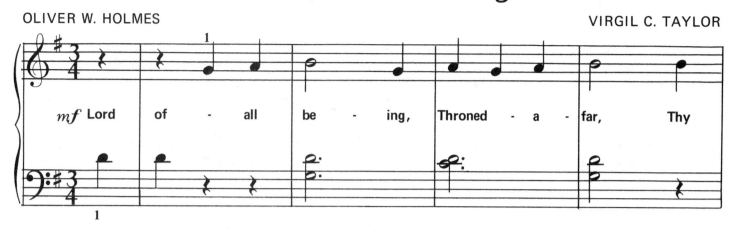

*mf* Lord of all be - ing, Throned - a - far, Thy

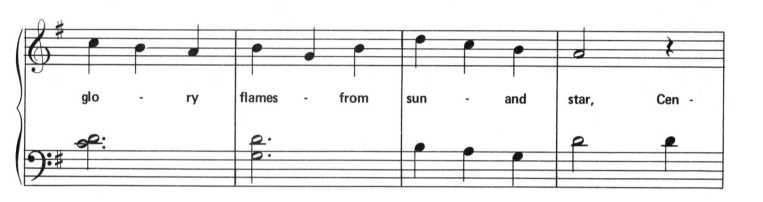

glo - ry flames - from sun - and star, Cen -

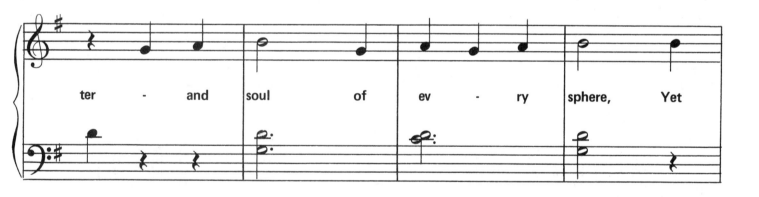

ter - and soul of ev - ry sphere, Yet

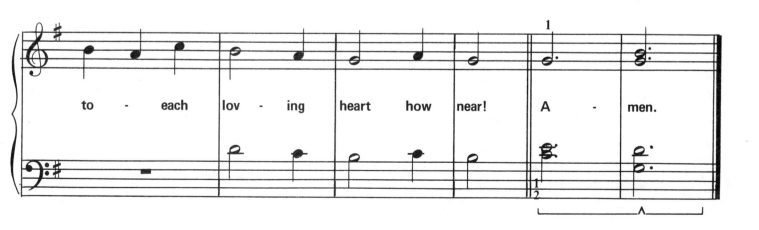

to - each lov - ing heart how near! A - men.

FDL 549

## Transposition

Playing music in a different key from which it is written is called TRANSPOSING. So far in this book you have learned to play in three major keys, C, F, and G. You should now go back and transpose the pieces written in the Key of C to the keys of F and G, the F pieces to C and G, and the G pieces to C and F. When you can transpose in these keys you should then play in other keys. On Pages 45 and 46 will be found transposition charts in the Major Keys of C, D, E, F, G, A and B. These are for reference should you need them. Eventually you should be able to transpose in all keys. This ability is necessary when you accompany singers. To play in the key that best suits the range of the voice often determines the success of a performance. When you have acquired the skills for transposing, you will be in great demand as a church musician.

# Exercises in Transposition

Using the Keyboard Charts on Pages 45 and 46, transpose the following exercises into seven major keys. An explanation of transposition will be found on these pages.

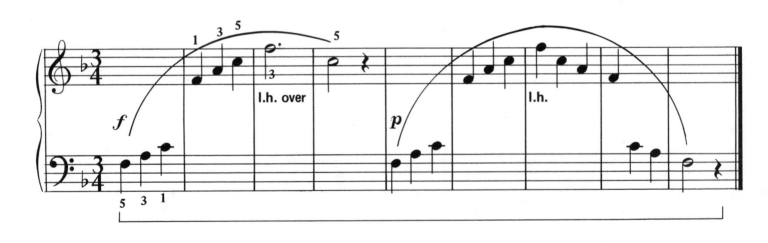

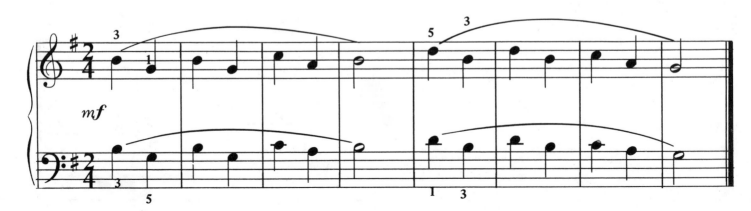

# Loving One Another

**When played with the Second Part, play both hands 8va higher.**

GLOVER

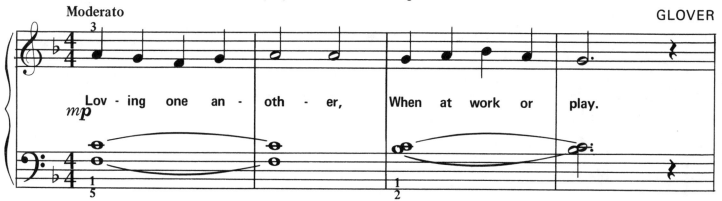

Lov - ing one an - oth - er, When at work or play.

Hap - py hearts to - geth - er, God has shown the way.

*rit.*

**Transpose *Loving One Another* into at least three other keys.**

## Second Part

### *Loving One Another*

*Con Pedal*

*rit.*

# Our Church Steeple

GLOVER

**Moderato**

The stee-ple of the church So state-ly in the sky. Is reach-ing for our God who watch-es from on high. Watch-es from on high Watch-es from on high.

*When the sign 8va is above notes it means to play 8 keys (octave) higher than written.

# Eighth Note and Eighth Rest

♪  **This is an EIGHTH NOTE.** It receives ½ of a Beat when the quarter note receives one beat. Two or more Eighth Notes are written like this -

Two **EIGHTH NOTES** ♫ = one Quarter Note ( ♩ ) and receive 1 Beat.

𝄾  **This is an EIGHTH REST.** It has the same time value as one Eighth Note.

Clap and Count ALOUD SLOWLY the following rhythm pattern.

Play and Count ALOUD SLOWLY. (Teacher: Clap basic rhythm while student plays and counts.)

---

**NOTE TO TEACHER:**
   Rather than go into lengthy detail on how to count rhythms containing eighth notes and eighth rests, the authors have left this to the discretion of the teacher.

Some favor counting ——————→ 1    &    2    &

others like ——————→ 1    a    2    a

still others ——————→ 1 - un    2 - oo    etc.

**This is a NATURAL** ♮ .   It cancels a Sharp ( ♯ ) or a Flat ( ♭ ).

*ff* **FORTISSIMO** — Very Loud

*pp* **PIANISSIMO** — Very Soft

# The Herald Angels

Animato (Lively)

GLOVER

You are now ready for a new solo GIVE ME THAT OLD TIME RELIGION.

FDL 549

## Accompanying

As an accompanist, in addition to being able to transpose music to keys other than written, the church musician should develop other skills which will make his performance more meaningful and interesting. When accompanying a congregation, play louder than when accompanying a soloist or a small group of people. Listen carefully as you accompany so that you may lend support to the singers rather than play so loudly that they cannot be heard. Also in accompanying a congregation, the accompanist must lead so that the tempo will not be too slow. However, when accompanying a soloist, the accompanist must follow rather than lead.

# *Fight The Good Fight With All Thy Might*

MONSELL

BOYD

# God Is Our Father

GLOVER

## Second Part
### God Is Our Father

**Both hands 8va higher.**

FDL 549

24

## Offertory

An Offertory is a composition played while the offering is being collected. It may be repeated, all or in part depending on how much time is needed. It is usually played at a moderate speed and not too loud.

## Cres.

**(CRESCENDO)** **gradually play louder**

## Dim.

**(DIMINUENDO)** **gradually play softer**

# *The Sound Of The Harp*
## Offertory

GLOVER

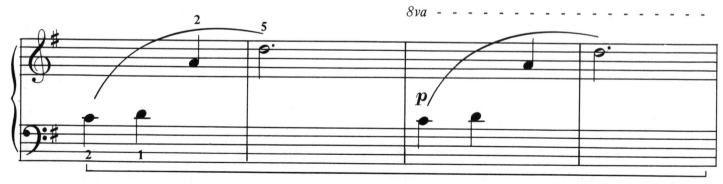

FDL 549

*When the sign 8va is below notes it means to play 8 keys (octave) lower than written.

---

### Doxology

The Doxology is a composition expressing praise to God. In many churches it is played and sung after the offering.

---

**Fermata**

Hold longer than the time value of the note.

# Praise God, From Whom All Blessings Flow

THOMAS KEN

## Doxology

LOUIS BOURGEOUS

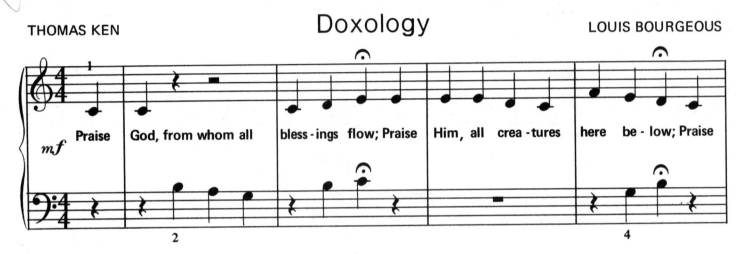

Praise God, from whom all bless-ings flow; Praise Him, all crea-tures here be-low; Praise

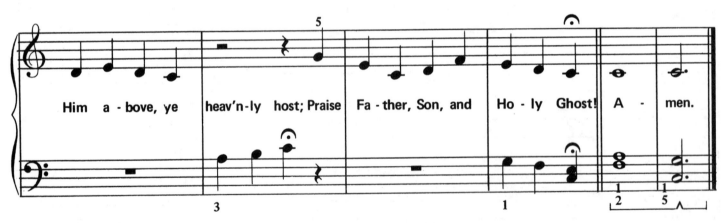

Him a-bove, ye heav'n-ly host; Praise Fa-ther, Son, and Ho-ly Ghost! A - men.

## Second Part
### Praise God, From Whom All Blessings Flow

Both hands 8va higher.

# When I Survey The Wondrous Cross

From a Gregorian Chant
Arr. by LOWELL MASON

ISAAC WATTS

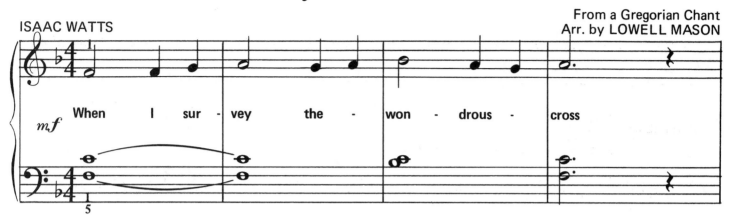

When I sur - vey the - won - drous - cross

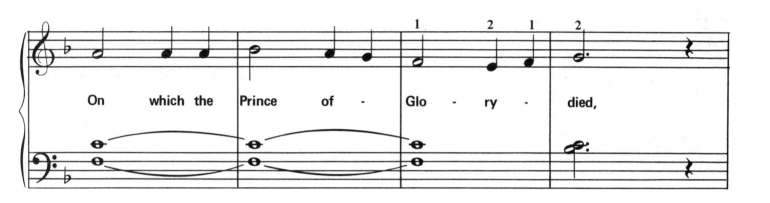

On which the Prince of - Glo - ry - died,

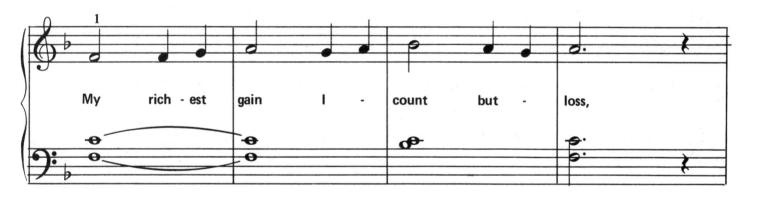

My rich - est gain I - count but - loss,

And pour con - tempt on all my - pride. A - men.

FDL 549

# Jesus, Thou Joy Of Loving Hearts

Bernard of Clair Vaux
Translated by RAY PALMER

HENRY BAKER

Je - sus, Thou Joy of lov - ing hearts,

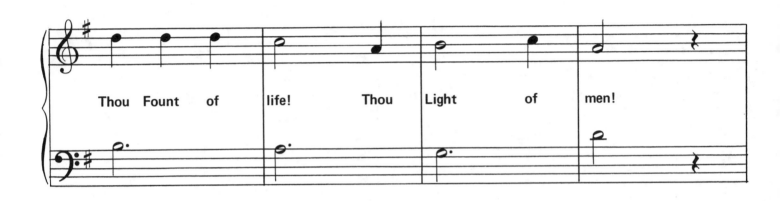

Thou Fount of life! Thou Light of men!

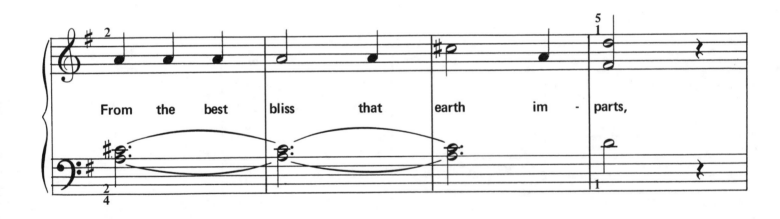

From the best bliss that earth im - parts,

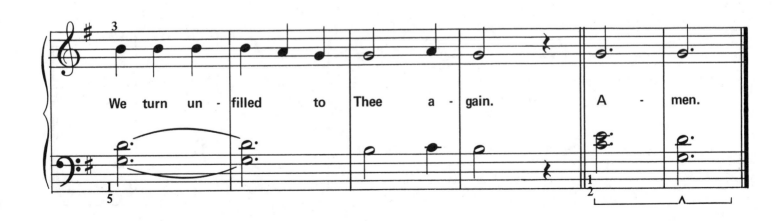

We turn un - filled to Thee a - gain. A - men.

FDL 549

# Bass Staff Notes

Lines

G B D F A

Spaces

A C E G

Write in the correct letter names of the following notes.

## Finger Patterns

### Left Hand

Jonah, a prophet of God, was asked by God to go to the people of Ninevah to preach and warn them that they must change their wicked ways or their city would be destroyed. Jonah did not know the people of this far-off city and refused to obey God's command. In order to escape, he boarded a ship going in the opposite direction from Ninevah. A great storm arose; and when the ship's crew realized that God had sent the storm because of Jonah, he was thrown over-board. A huge fish swallowed Jonah, and there he remained in the belly of the fish for three days. Jonah prayed asking God's forgiveness and promised to do as he had been commanded. The fish then came to shore and with one great cough threw Jonah on the beach. Immediately he went to Ninevah preaching and warning the people of God's promise to destroy them if they did not change. The people listened and believed so God forgave their sins and Ninevah was spared.

# Jonah In The Whale

GLOVER

Andante (walking speed)

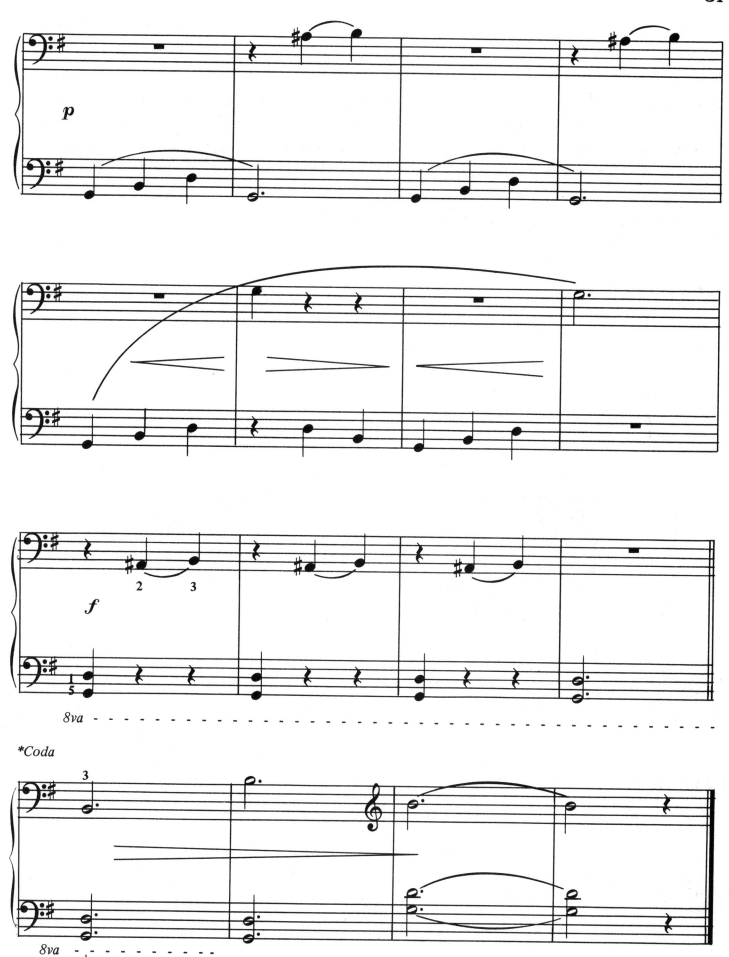

*Coda*

**Coda** is an Italian word for "tail". It is used in music to describe any passage added to a composition to make it sound more complete.

FDL 549

## Introduction

Usually the accompanist plays an introduction before the congregation sings. A form of introduction is to play through the entire hymn once. This is an excellent way for the congregation to become familiar with a new hymn before singing. It also allows time to find the music in the hymnal. Other suggestions for an introduction to the hymn below are: 1. play the first eight measures ending on the third beat of measure eight; 2. play the last eight measures beginning on the fourth beat of the preceding measure; 3. play the last four measures beginning on the fourth beat of the preceding measure.

# *This Is My Father's World*

MALTIE D. BABCOCK

TRADITIONAL ENGLISH MELODY

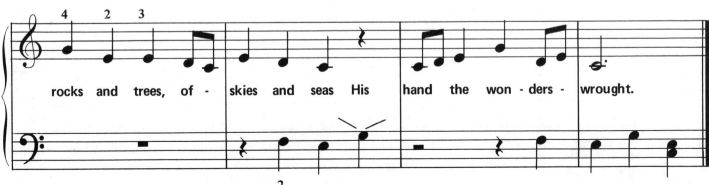

# Treble Staff Notes

Lines

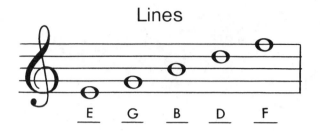

E G B D F

Spaces

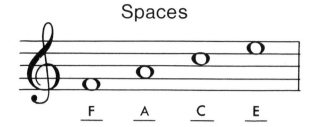

F A C E

**Write in correct letter names of the following notes.**

— — — — — — — — — —

— — — — — — — — — —

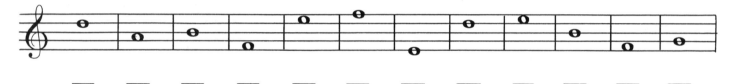

— — — — — — — — — —

— — — — — — — — — —

# Finger Patterns

## Right Hand

# *Heavenly Stars*
## Bass Part

Heavenly Stars may be played as a solo using Treble First Player part only, or as a trio which would be played by three performers each using one of the parts given. When played as a trio, Treble First and Second players wait for a four-measure Introduction at the beginning and a four-measure Coda at the end played by the Bass Player.

# Heavenly Stars
## (Twinkle Twinkle Little Star)
### Treble First Part (Solo)

Play this part 2 octaves higher when Treble Second Part is used.

Stems up r.h.
Stems down l.h.

## Heavenly Stars

### Treble Second Part

Stems up r.h.
Stems down l.h.

*Hold this note until the Bass Player has completed the Coda.

FDL 549

# Our Great Saviour

J. WILBUR CHAPMAN

ROWLAND W. PRITCHARD

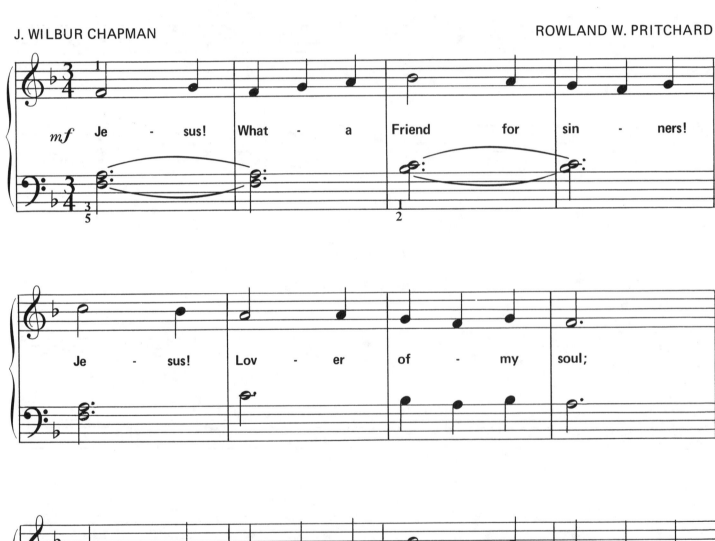

*mf* Je - sus! What - a Friend for sin - ners!

Je - sus! Lov - er of - my soul;

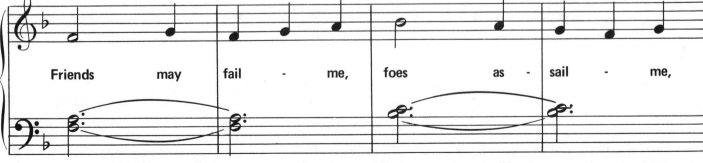

Friends may fail - me, foes as - sail - me,

FDL 549

## Background Music

On occasions background music is used in a religious service such as during the Pastor's Prayer or Holy Communion. It is always played softly. The following solo "Prayer" is in the Key Of A Minor which you will learn more about later.

# Prayer

GLOVER

FDL 549

**Da Capo al Fine means return to the beginning
and play to the "FINE" (pronounced fee-nay).**

## Second Part

*Prayer*

**Both hands 8va higher.**

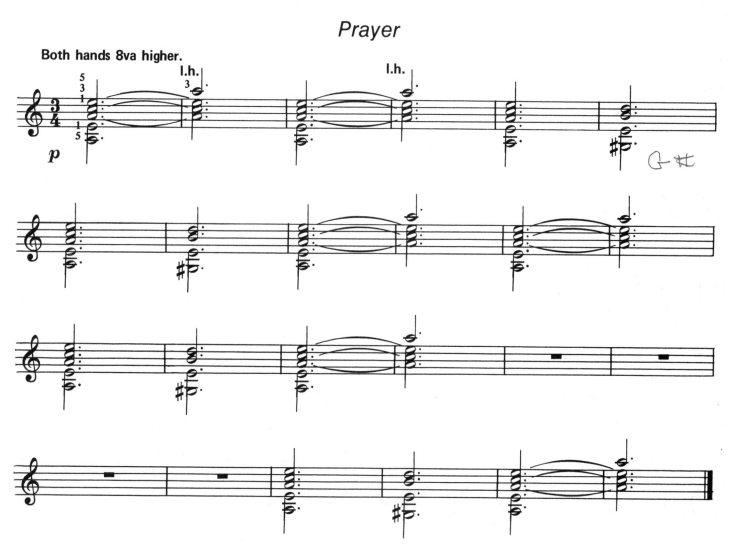

A Postlude is a composition usually played as the congregation leaves the church at the close of the worship service. If all the people have not left the church at the end of the Postlude, continue to play by repeating all or part of the piece.

ACCENT MARK > — Play Loudly

GLOVER

You are now ready for a new solo HE'S GOT THE WHOLE WORLD IN HIS HANDS.

# Music For Special Days
## THANKSGIVING
### *Now Thank We All Our God*

MARTIN RINKART                                    JOHANN CRUGER

# CHRISTMAS

## *Jesus, In The Manger*
### Bass Part

**Stems up r.h.**
**Stems down l.h.**
**Slowly**
**Introduction**

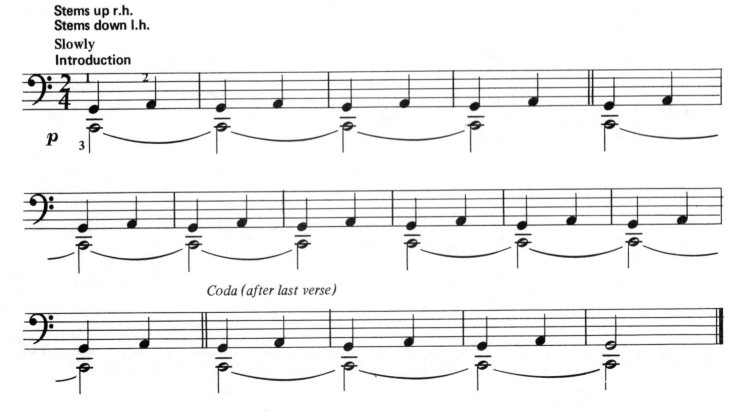

*Coda (after last verse)*

# Jesus, In The Manger
## Treble First Part (Solo)

GLOVER

Slowly

I. Ti - ny ba - by Je - sus sleep - ing in the hay,

*mf*

Glo - ry, Glo - ry, Al - le - lu - ia, This is Christ - mas day.

*f*

2. Animals around him
   They won't go away,
   Glory, Glory, Alleluia
   This is Christmas day.

3. Joseph stands in silence
   Mary softly prays,
   Glory, Glory, Alleluia
   This is Christmas day.

4. Tiny baby Jesus
   Sleeping in the hay,
   Glory, Glory, Alleluia
   This is Christmas day.

## *Jesus, In The Manger*

### Treble Second Part

Stems up r.h. — Stems down l.h.
Slowly — Introduction
Both hands 8va higher throughout.

*p*

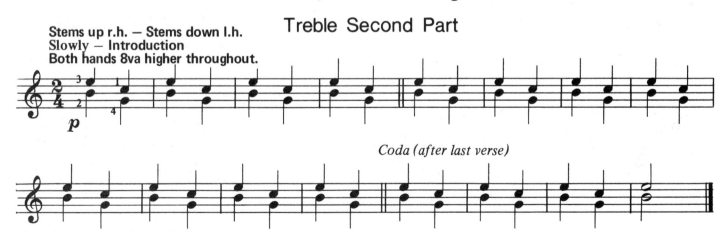

*Coda (after last verse)*

Jesus In The Manger can be played as a solo (omit Bass Player and Treble Second Player Parts); as a duet (use only one of the other two parts given); and as a trio (use all parts given). When played as a duet or trio, First Player (solo) waits for a four-measure introduction. This may also be done before each stanza.

# EASTER
## *Alleluia*

GLOVER

## Transposition

You have learned that playing music in a different key from that in which it is written is called TRANS-POSING. The pieces in this book can be transposed to all keys. Below are six keyboard charts and left hand accompaniment intervals showing the correct five-finger position in the Major Keys of C, D, E, F, G, A and B. These charts are intended for reference and are to be used at the discretion of the teacher. For the more mature student it is suggested that all three notes of the I and V7 chords be used. These three note chords are presented in Level II of The Church Musician.

## C Major

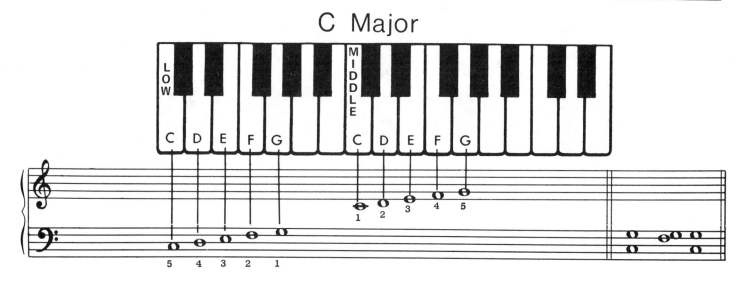

## D Major

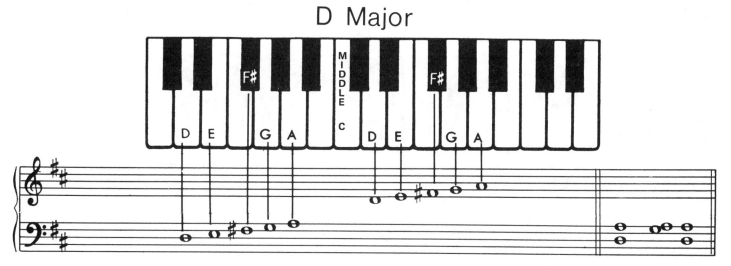

## E Major

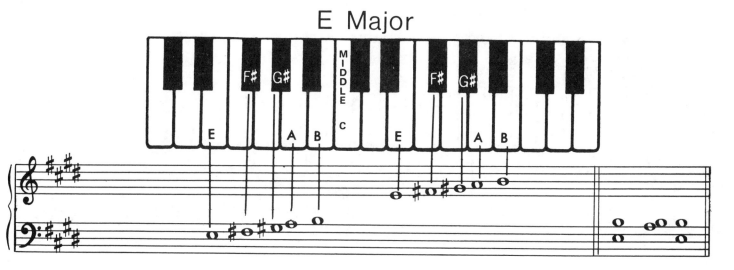

# F Major

## G Major

## A Major

## B Major

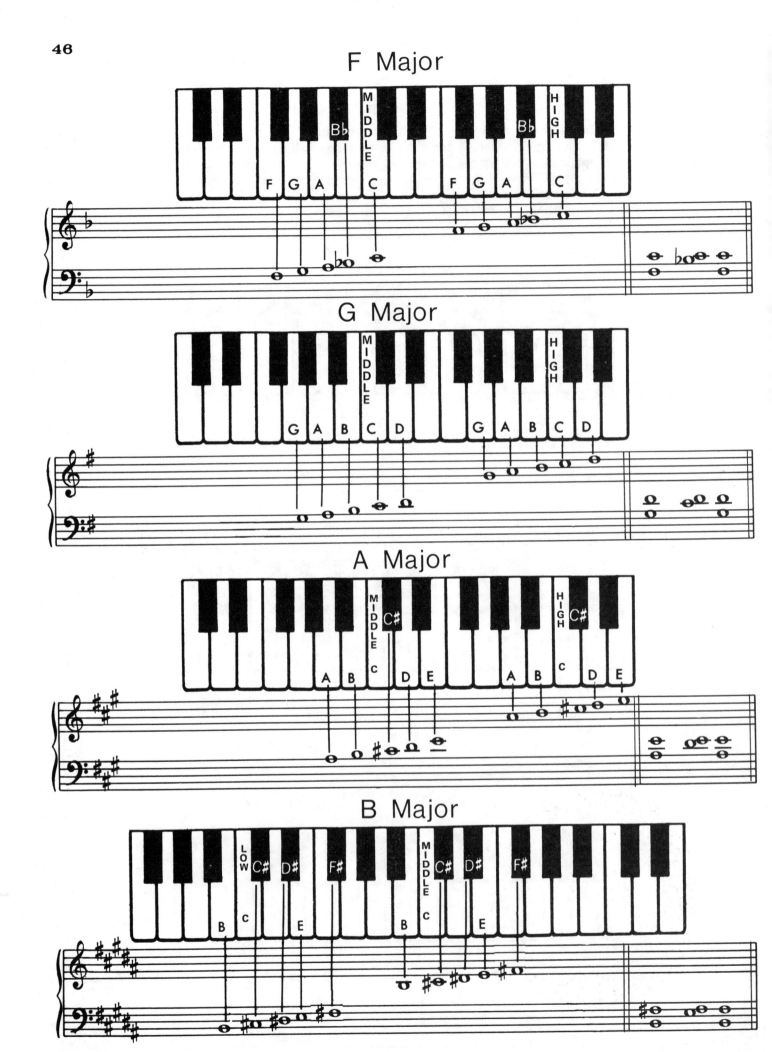

FDL 549

# Certificate of Award

*This is to certify that*

*has completed*

# The Church Musician Method
## Level One

*of the*

### David Carr Glover
### Christian Piano Library

_____
DATE

_____
TEACHER